ChoiceAphorismsfromtheSeven SegmentsofCardan

William Lilly

Contents

GeneralAphorisms

1.　　LIFE is short, Art long, Experience not easily obtained, Judgement difficult, and therefore it is necessary, that a Student not only exercise himself in considering several Figures, but also that he diligently read the writings of others who have treated rationally of this Science, and make it his business to find out the true natural causes of things by experiments, to know the certain places and processions of tee Planets and Fixed Stars, Constellations, etc., but above all to be a passionate lover of truth.

2.　　The Principles of Art are three, Reason, Sense, and Experience, but the Principles of Operations four, viz: The Planets, The Parts of Heaven, The Fixed Stars, and the Site or Position of all those in respect of one another.

3.　　There are some things perfectly known, as the Circle of Ascension, some in a competent measure, as the Revolution of the Sun; some may be known although they yet are not, as the Revolution of the Superiors; some things fall under knowledge, yet cannot be exactly known, as the precise Ingress of the Sun into the Equinoctial Point; some are neither known, nor can be known, as the complete commixtures and distinct virtues of all the Stars.

4. It is much w　orse for an Artist to conceive he knows those things, which he is ignorant of, than to be ignorant of those things which he ought to know.

5.　　Mean learning with an excellent judgement, avails more than a mean judgement with the greatest learning, :yet is judgement very much assisted and perfected by learning: but everything prospers better, and is far more easily perfected that has nature for its guide and favourable stars, than that which is attempted by human industry though never so diligent.

6.   He that has too great a conceit of himself will be apt to fall into many errors in his judgement; yet on the other side, he that is too diffident, is not fit for this Science.

7.   He that would truly promote Art must insist as much on the confutation of false opinions delivered by others, as in the declaration of truth.

8.   An Astrologer is so far only true and honest, as he depends in his conjectures on principles of natural philosophy, and since those Arts which are inherent in their proper subjects, cannot promise any certainty concerning matters to come, the Astrologer ought never to pronounce anything absolutely or peremptorily of future contingencies,

9.   Truths of themselves are to be desired, for Science itself is a certain good, now the expectation of future good very much delights us, and on the contrary, when future evils are foreseen, we may either avoid them, mitigate them, or at least bear them more contentedly.

10.   Heaven is the instrument of the most High God, whereby he acts upon, and governs inferior things.

11.   He that asserts thin~ that can never be proved by experience is deceived and ambitious, but thus it always happens, those that are most ignorant of Art delight to boast of doing things difficult or wonderful.

12.   It is all one as to promoting of Art, etc., and the knowledge thereof, either from Nativities known, to predict what shall happen, or after accidents have happened, to discover the Nativities before

unknown which are thereby rectified but as to vulgar opinion, the first way far exceeds the last.

13.   He that goes about to destroy Art, is far worse than he that is unskilled in it, for his mind is full of malice and idleness as well as ignorance.

14.   Men may be said almost to be compelled by the Stars, even in voluntary actions, by means of their corrupt affections and ignorance.

15.   Always deliver judgements from the Stars in general terms, or if thou dost otherwise let it be when thou hast very evident testimonies and in great and weighty matters.

16.   We ought not to use arguments or tedious discourses in giving judgement, much less flatteries, but only to pronounce what is known by experience and firm reason.

17.   A main reason why events are so rarely foretold by Astrologers, is because the Art is yet but imperfectly discovered, for hitherto those that have been most excellent in

it, being commonly old persons, have despaired to live to see the fortunes of children newly-born, and the Nativities of persons grown up, being uncertain, they scarce thought them worth so much labour.

18.   When true genitures exactly taken in accidents prove false or absurd, and not agreeable to the things signified, they are to be accounted monstrous, and are to be avoided as anatomists do monstrous bodies in their dissections; for they overthrow Art,

19.   Generals are to be gathered from Singulars, and Singulars from Generals, and an Artist ought always to learn to distinguish between that which is by itself, and that which is only by accident.

20. The str ength and efficacy of Fixed Stars is to be considered from their magnitude, their splendours, their natures or properties, their

nearness to the Ecliptic, their place in the World, their multitude, their first oriental appearance, the purity of their place, the similitude or agreement of the body or rays of a Planet with them and their circle of position.

21.   The Light of the time is the Sun in the day, and morning twilight; and the Moon in the night when she is above the Earth, and in her morning rising: so that sometimes there may be two lights of the time, sometimes it so happens that th6re is none.

22.   When a Planet is within five degrees of the cusp of any house, it shall be accounted to have virtue in that house though actually posited behind the cusp in another house.

23. Not only Trines and Sextiles may be counted friendly aspects, but even Squares and Oppositions too, if there happen a Reception.

Aphorisms Relating To Nativities

1.   A Child is then said to be born when first it breathes in air at its mouth, when outside its mother's womb.

2.   Those that have the Luminaries unfortunate in Angles will be apt to commit suicide.

3.   Those that have Saturn in Opposition to Jupiter, will never enjoy peace, and those that have the Dragon's Tail with Jupiter, will seldom be rich.

4.   Those that have Saturn and Mars in the same part of the Zodiac will be liable, in the course of their lives, to many misfortunes; and if they shall both be in Taurus, and posited in the fourth house; when the Ascendant, by direction, comes to their rays, the Natives will have some severe falls, or be in danger by reason of some ruinous buildings failing on them.

5.   Fixed Signs give learning; with the exception of Scorpio; Common Signs, manners and conversation, with the exception of Virgo, and Moveable Signs, riches; with the exception of Capricorn; whence it appears that those are bad nativities that have all the Planets in Virgo, Scorpio or Capricorn.

6.   If the Ascendant be one of those Signs called "Mute," and Mercury in one that is not humane, with any fixed Star of the nature of Saturn, the Native will never speak well, but bring forth his words with difficulty.

7.   He that hath the Moon in Taurus in the second separating from the Square or Opposition of Jupiter, and applying to Trine of the Sun shall obtain very considerable riches.

8.   When the Abscissor, cutter off of life, or killing Planet is on the Ecliptic, and an Infortune in an Angle, the Native will die a violent death.

9.   When an Infortune is posited on the cusp of the seventh house, the Native will be liable to great calamities, and if an Infortune be in Aspect with the Sun or Moon afflicted in the same place, the Native, though a Prince, shall suffer a world of troubles.

10.   Aries ascending, signifies the Natives to be handsome, and of a grave composed temper, but Scorpio on the horoscope, notes them to be great liars.

11.   When the Moon is in Scorpio in Square of Saturn in Leo, or in Opposition to him when he is partially in Taurus, the Native rarely has either wife or children. If Saturn be in Aquarius, he will be a mere woman-hater.

12.   If the Dragon's Tail be with Saturn in Square of the Moon, and she Cadent, the Native will be consumptive, especially if from an Angle; but if besides it be in Square to the Lord of the Ascendant, he will be sickly and infirm all the days of his life, and if such Aspect happen in or from the sixth house, so much the worse.

13.   When Jupiter is in the Sixth house, Retrograde, and the Lord of the Second Peregrine, and no benevolent fixed star to help, the Native will be very poor and necessitous.

14.   He that has Mars in his Ascendant shall be exposed to many dangers, and commonly receives, at some time, a great scar or cut, on his face.

15.   Mercury mixing his beams with Mars, is a great argument of a violent death.

16.   If Jupiter and the Moon in any nativity shall be very weak and afflicted though other positions seem never so promising, yet the

Native shall be exceedingly unhappy.

17.   When Venus is with Saturn and beholds the Lord of the Ascendant, the Native is inclined to Sodomy, or at least shall love old hard favoured women, or poor dirty wenches.

18.   When Venus and Jupiter shall be in the Seventh, the Moon beholding them in her own dignities, and the Dragon's Head joined with them or with Mercury, the Native shall get a great Estate by means of his wives.

19.   The Moon full of light in Conjunction with Mars, makes the Native to be counted a fool; but if she be void of light and with Saturn, he is so indeed.

20.   Venus in the heart of the Sun gives vast honours and dignities, the same may be hoped for, if a Planet with the Fixed Star called "Cor Leonis," behold the Moon.

21.   The Moon in the Seventh house renders Natives subject to the Falling-sickness, and sometimes when she is in the Ascendant, but generally she makes them fools if she be afflicted

22.   Bastards and supposititious children have frequently the Ascendant in aspect with the Moon, and not the significator of the Father; and for the most part attended with indications of some great misfortunes, and either there is no agreement between the Lord of the fourth, the Lord of the second and the Moon, or else Venus is joined with Mars or Mercury.

23.   When Jupiter shall be in the tenth in Trine of Mars, and strong; and the Sun with the Dragon's Head, and the Moon with Cor Leonis; such Native, though the son of the meanest peasant, shall be wonderfully exalted.

24.   When any Planet shall be partly on the cusp of the Seventh in his own house, the Native's death will be of the nature of that Planet

and Place.

25.   The Infortunes in Angles denote a public death or a sudden one; the Sun there, afflicted, it shall be by some weapon, or burning~ the Moon, by hanging, or drowning, according to circumstances.

26.   Sol and Mars peregrine or the Dragon's Tail in the Second, signifies that the Native shall squander away his substance or Estate foolishly.

27.   When the Moon in Opposition to the Sun is joined with nebulous stars, the Native will have some defect in his sight; if the Moon in the Seventh be afflicted by both the Infortunes, and if their rays are very strong he will be blind.

28.   The compound rays of Jove, Venus, Mercury, and the Moon, give the greatest grace and sweetness of speech, and therefore when Jupiter shall be in Virgo, and the Moon in Pisces, it is an opportune time for the birth of a Poet. Poets are always born, not made.

29.   That person will scarce make a prosperous end, or persevere long in any eminent degree, who has not some of his Ancestors' Genitures to sympathise with, and assist his own.

30.   The fifth sign from the Ascendant signifies the Native's children, because it is of the same nature as the sign on the Ascendant, and if two signs shall be in the Ascendant, the children will be of humours and manners exceedingly different, the one from the other; for the same reason the ninth house, signifies grand-children.

31.   The Moon with the Dragon's Tail in a Nativity gives suspicion of the mother's honesty, and hints that the child is none of the reputed father's begetting; however, it will prove ill-mannered, and for the most part unfortunate.

32.   Whoever has Jupiter in aspect with the Sun, will be proud and haughty, and yet shall have little cause for it, unless they happen to be in reception.

33.   The Nativities of women in matters appertaining to life, are like those of men, but as to fortune, wholly unlike, and touching manners, after a middle kind, neither wholly agreeable, nor wholly contrary.

34.   A woman that has Mars with the Moon is right; I'll warrant her.

35.   In complete Nativities the Moon returns to the sign ascending at conception, or its opposite, or to the body or aspect of some Planet with whom she was at the conception, or to her own sign, and generally the Ascendant at birth is the Moon's place at conception, or its opposite, or the place of the Lord of the New Moon foregoing the conception, yet there are sober genitures too, when the Sun comes to the place of the Ascendant or its Lord, etc.

36.   When Mars or the Moon shall be with the Dragon's Head or Tail in the twelfth, and Sol and Jupiter in the fourth house, the Native will be hunch-backed.

37.   When Mars is Lord of a Woman's Ascendant, and Venus posited in it, or Venus is Lady of it, and Mars in it, or Mars Lord of the Ascendant in the mid-heaven; it is more than probable she will Cuckold her husband.

38.   The Lord of the Ascendant in the combust way, shows that the Native will be much entangled and pestered with business.

39.   If Infortunes be in the tenth house, peregrine, and not friendly to the Ascendant, the Native will be always full of suspicions and jealousies.

40.   All Planets above the Earth, make a man illustrious and generally known far and near, and being all swift in motion, render him dexterous and nimble in the dispatch of affairs.

41.   Those that have the Moon, Lady of the Ascendant under the Earth, with the "Tail of the Lion ," and the "Virgin's Head," the Sun in the sixth, and Saturn or Mars in their own dignities in the Angles of the seventh, will always be very infirm and weak.

42.   Mercury in Pisces lays an impediment on the tongue, making a man absurd in his speech and uttering unawares what he does not conceive in his mind; so if that sign ascend.

43.   Whoever is born on the day of the Vernal Equinox at noon, shall by that testimony alone, become great in the world.

44.   Women that have their Ascendant, Moon, Mars, Venus, and Mercury in double-bodied signs, have generally very evil qualities.

45.   Jupiter very potent in a geniture always promises some extraordinary happiness~ and if he be in the Mid-heaven near the cusp in Capricorn he gives a great deal of good fortune by means of violence and power under pretence of justice, but the same will have an unfortunate issue.

46.   Famous are those persons in whose Nativities the Moon receives the light of many Planets, or is joined to some powerful Royal Fixed Star.

47.   When Sol and Jupiter rule in the ninth, and over the places of Mercury, the Moon, and Ascendant, and do behold each other, such a Native's words will be regarded as oracles.

48.   Jupiter and the Sun in the second house, give a gallant, noble, free spirit; but Saturn and Mars, or Saturn with Mercury in the seventh, render men sordidly covetous.

49.   When the Lord of the figure of a Nativity shall be Retrograde, and both ways Cadent; the Native will be a weak poor-spirited, dejected fellow, bringing nothing to perfection.

50.   An Artist may more easily and certainly judge of a man's Nativity, than of the weather, because he knows the time of birth, but not that of the gathering together of vapours.

51.   Sol in Leo alone raises a man, at least scarce ever suffers him to want or beg; and if the same sign ascend, it buoys up his spirit with hopes, and makes him master of more than ordinary reason.

52.   If Cancer ascend, and the Moon be in Moveable or Common signs, especially remote from an Angle, the Native is credulous, light, and inconstant.

53.   Venus in the house or exaltation of Mars is always a sign of filthy lust.

54.   The Moon in Aquarius or Pisces makes the Native to be disliked by Princes, Grandees and the upper ten.

55.   When the Lord of the Mid-heaven separates by Retrogradation from the Lord of the Ascendant, the Prince, King, or Ruler, shall be averse to the Native, but if on the other side the Lord of the Ascendant being Retrograde forsakes the Lord of the tenth, then the Native shall hate his Prince, King, or Governors; the like is to be understood of other houses according to their respective significations.

56.   A Native of a City having the same sign and degree ascending with that City, shall in that place, by that alone grow great and eminent.

57.   When the Lord of the second applies to the Lord of the Ascendant; especially if that Lord of the Ascendant be Jupiter; the

Native shall, all his lifetime, be happy in acquiring riches even to admiration.

58.   When the Lord of the Ascendant beholds the Sun with a friendly aspect or is Oriental next to the Sun, or joined with the Lord of the tenth, the Native will be much beloved by Kings and great people; for the cause of which favour consider the nature of the said Lord of the Ascendant and his place.

59.   When several children have the same accidents and fortune, if it be in their childhood, it may be shown by the genitures of their parents; or if in their old age, we may conclude the Nativities of their Parents were so powerful that they assimilate their Nativities between themselves and suit them to the disposition of Children in the Paternal Figure.

60.   Mars in moveable Signs makes people hasty and choleric, but nowhere more than in Cancer, nor less than in Virgo, but in the former he generally makes the tongue more foolish and impertinent.

61.   Saturn in the Twelfth threatens the gout; in the Sixth some lasting disease or tedious imprisonments.

62.   If the Moon be between Mars and Sol or with them, the Native will almost exchange his cradle for a grave, being very short-lived.

63.   If the Moon separates from an Infortune, the Native will suffer many diseases in nursing, and afflictions afterwards.

64.   Whoever has Venus not well posited; within the rays of Mars, unfortunate, will assuredly suffer a world of mischief and troubles by means of love."

65.   Watery Signs; but especially, and above all others, Scorpio, make traitors; and therefore if the Moon Lady of the Ascendant be in that viperous sign; the Native will betray, or prove a traitor to, his

master; and if the same position happen in the radix of a city, its inhabitants will be rebellious against their Princes or Governors.

66.　　Mars is seldom joined with Mercury for good, for he makes people naughty and impudent, yet industrious in Art, whence it comes to pass that the best Artists are too often the worst men.

67. Mar s unfortunate in the Ninth, signifies liars and atheists.

68.　　He that has Mercury well posited but the Moon afflicted shall understand well, but deliberate ill, and therefore such, though they may advise others excellent]y, yet shall manage their own affairs foolishly.

69.　　When Venus shall be too powerful in a geniture, and in places of the Infortunes, inconveniences are to be feared from unlawful loves.

70.　　When the Moon and Mercury, and Lord of the Ascendant shall be all in double-bodied Signs, the Native will be naturally addicted to old opinions and curious religious notions.

71.　　When Saturn and Mars behold each other, and the Luminaries be posited in the sixth, eighth, or twelfth houses, the Native shall labour under some incurable disease and lead a life wholly miserable.

72.　　When the Moon is in the Mid-heaven in Capricorn, and Saturn or Mars in the fourth, the Native will be infamous, and so much the worse if Mars be in Taurus, and the Moon in Scorpio, for then many troubles will attend him during his whole life.

73.　　When Venus is with Saturn and Mars, and in opposition to the place of the Moon, the Native shall be but m fool, yet think himself a Philosopher.

74.　　For the profession or Art of the Native we must consider the Planet which being Oriental first makes its egress from under the

Sun beams, and if with this there be another in the Mid-heaven that beholds the Moon, take him for an Assistant, but if there be no such Planet coming from under the Sun beams take him that is in the mid-heaven, and if there be none therein posited then the Lord of it, and the places of Mars, Venus, and Mercury, but when these happen to be many, the Native will practise several Arts; now the Art a Native practises is much affected by the series of revolutions, which if they agree with his Nativity, he will be delighted with it; otherwise he will do it against his will.

75.   A prime cause of men leading single lives is the combustion of the Moon in their Nativities with Saturn, or eminently afflicted by him, so in women if a Planet be combust or the Sun in Taurus greatly afflicted,

76.   Mars and Mercury evilly disposed, and in conjunction with the Moon, signifies Thieves and Robbers, but if Saturn behold them, or be in the Seventh, they will suffer according to their deserts, and therefore whenever you see indications of grievous crimes, consider whether the Infortunes are strong or not, and oppress the Sun, Moon, or Lord of the Ascendant; or if the Lord of the Ascendant be combust, or in an enemy to the Moon, for then undoubtedly the Native will suffer for his Villainy.

77.   When the Moon is joined to Saturn in an Angle, the Native though a grandee will be reduced to poverty.

78.   Let him that has Mars in the second house beware of concerning himself in merchandise.

79.   He that hath a Nativity unfortunate for riches and honour, and yet the Moon in conjunction with an eminent propitious fixed star, shall unexpectedly become potent, and again fall to misery, but to judge of the greatness of the event consider the state of the Moon.

80.   When Venus is in the eleventh, Mercury in the twelfth, the Sun in the horoscope, Jupiter in the second, Saturn in the sixth and the Moon in the ninth, so many and great accidents will happen to he Native that his life may justly be esteemed prodigious.

81.   Saturn, Mars and the Dragon's Head in the fourth, betokens sudden death.

82.   When the Moon in a nocturnal Geniture passes by her beams from Mars to Saturn, many inconveniences will happen to he Native, chiefly associated with women.

83.   Those persons are like to prove very learned in whose Nativities Saturn, Venus, Jupiter and the Moon, do exactly behold Mercury, provided that neither Saturn nor the moon be posited in the Ascendant, and that there be no planet in an angle, for any planet strong in an Angle is an impediment to wisdom.

84.   When the Sun peregrine in "Corde Coeli" shall be in square of the Moon in the Seventh, the Native will come to be the chief of his family or faction, but shall die suddenly.

85.   I all Nativities examine exactly all the Moon's conditions in relations to the three ways whereby she is exalted for 'tis very necessary.

86.   When Infortunes are in Angles and Fortunes in Succedent houses, or the Moon combust, and the Lord of her place strong and happy, or Jupiter Cadent and his disposition well dignified:- the Native from a sad mean condition and great misery shall rise to a considerable grandeur and felicity, and so on the contrary.

87.   When the Moon Venus and Mars are altogether in conjunction, 'tis a fit time to bring Neros and such cursed monsters of mankind into the world: the Native's manners are prodigiously wicked.

88.   Jupiter elevated and a little infortunated, destroys the natives children but preserves his estate:- if he be descending and low and not unfortunate, he gives children but not an estate.

89.   When Saturn does not threaten a violent death, yet if he be in, or lord of the seventh or eighth houses he signifies the Native shall die from Grief of the mind.

90.   Infortunes peregrine in the seventh house, having dominions in the Ascendant, denotes the deaths of the Native's wives or enemies.

91.   It is next to impossible that they that have never a planet above the earth, nor in the Ascendant of their nativities should either live long or accomplish any great matters in the world.

92.   The number of a Native's wives (where only one at once is lawful) is to be found out not only from the Concourse of the planets or Common signs, but with that you must consider that fit applications of the Moon to planets at ripe years and testimonies of the Death of Wives do also concur.

93.   When Mars or Mercury afflict the Lord of the Seventh, being elevated above him, the Native will kill his wife or his enemy, even though it be wit poison, especially if either of them have power in the Ascendant.

94.   In a woman's Nativity Mars shall be under the Sun's Beams, she will be apt to play the Harlot with her servants and mean fellows but if Venus be true, then she will trade discreetly with Nobles and gallants of quality.

95.   Infortunes afflicting the place of children, if they be but a little weak, the Native may have children, if much debilitated, the children he has will die, if they be very weak he be wholly barren.

96.   When the Lord of the Geniture in an Infortune and does not behold the place of children, or being a fortune beholds them with

an aspect of hatred, the native will never love his children as he ought to do.

97.   When Mercury is under the earth he has greater efficacy in relation to giving Arts and Sciences, but in respect of eloquence he is best when he is above the earth.

98.   When Mars is exactly on the cusp of the Mid-heaven and has no dominion in the Ascendant if the Native live to any considerable age, 'tis much to be feared that he will be killed.

99.   When it happens that the Significators of persons of quality well posited in their own genitures, are such as were unfortunate in the Nativities of their Parents, it signifies that they shall spin out a laborious life as to riches and honours to a considerable age, and then by successive increases, shall attain to great Estates and Eminence, whence 'tis evident that the lives of no persons may be more unlikely to each other, than theirs who were born at the same time.

100.   Nativities that can never be good, are such as have both the Infortunes in the same place joined to one of the Luminaries, or when infortunes single are singly joined to the Luminaries, or when the Moon is under sun beams with Saturn or Mars, or where all the planets are in the third, sixth, eighth and twelfth houses; or when the Infortunes are in Angles, and the Luminaries and Fortunes cadent, or when the Luminaries only are cadent and all the other planets Retrograde, or when both Luminaries and both Fortunes are afflicted, or when only Mars is above the earth the other planets not being mutually joined nor in Angles.

AphorismsConcerning Revolutions

1.Revolutions   may be said to be accomplished five ways, first by the return of the Sun yo the same point, which is most valid. Secondly the return of the centre of a planet to the same place of the Ecliptic, of which kind that of the Moon first and then those of Saturn and Jupiter are chief. Thirdly the return of the centre of some smaller Circle to the same place. Fifthly the return of a planet wherewith he was in the beginning joined as it is the place of another Planet.

2.   When the Dragon's Tail in a Nativity unfortunately beholds the Lord of the Ascendant and in a revolution the Moon shall be joined therewith, and the Lord of the House of Death being then in the place of an Infortune in the radix, shall likewise behold it, the Party that year will die.

3.   When the Infortunes are strong in the Radix, and the Moon applies to a powerful fixed star of the nature of Mars in a Revolution, the Party will be apt to commit manslaughter that year or be in danger about it.

4.   Revolutions may produce effects happening in the years following, wither because ones year is preparative to another, or because the Nativity decrees what the Revolution perfects, or by reason of greatness of the event as death, or of the causes, as when the Sun is exactly in opposition to Jupiter

5.   When the Ascendant of a Revolution is the same with that of the Person's Nativity, something promised in the geniture happens, but more certainly if the Moon shall be also in her place of the geniture,

or the Lord of the Ascendant in a place partially behold the same house of the Radix.

6.   If in a Revolution the Lord of the Geniture Retrograde (if he be one of the Inferiors) begins to be under the sun's beams, or (if he be one of the Superiors) if he be afflicted by an Infortune, you may expect some danger of your life that year.

7.   When Jupiter in a Revolution beholds the Moon or Venus, or be in an angle in either of their places in the Radix, it inclines the Party, if of fit age that year, to marry.

8.   When in a person's Revolution whose only significator of life was debilitated in the Radix, the Fortunes shall be combust in any house but the Ascendant, and the Infortunes being above the earth, shall behold the Sun Ascendant and Moon, or the Moon be under the earth, such person without any ill direction may die that year.

9.   If a Geniture we weak as to life, and three planets be joined in a Revolution, there is imminent danger of some eminent disease, especially if they happen in the 6thhouse .

10.   When at ripe age, a Revolution shall have Venus in sextile of Mercury, who was joined to her in the Genesis in the same place, the native will be strangely haunted with wanton thoughts and venereal imaginations, and if they shall be in conjunction in the same place where before they were in sextile, he shall that year enjoy some mistress that he is much enamoured of.

11. When in the hour of a Revolution the Superior Planets or others shall b joined in the place of a Radical Significator, expect from thence some notable matter to happen of that kind which is thereby naturally promised.

12.   When the Moon is joined with Saturn in a Revolution, and he casts a square to the Ascendant, such person shall that year suffer in

his body by reason of a disease of his mind.

13.   The additions that are made by the procession of the sun in an annual Revolution, transfer the significations for near upon so many days after the Revolution as there are years past.

14.   When the Moon agreeing with Saturn in the Radix, or being with any other Planet in his dignities, if she happen in a Revolution (after the age of forty years) to be corporally joined with Saturn in the same latitude, or being full of light shall be in opposition to him and in contrary latitude from the sixth house to the eighth, the Native will undoubtedly fall into some strange disease and die thereof.

15.   When the houses of the Ascendant or Moon in the Radix shall be in square or opposition to the Infortunes in a Revolution, the Native will suffer much trouble, but if the Moon be in conjunction with them, then he shall do much mischief to other people, but if besides this the Infortunes are Lords of inimical places, He shall both do damage to others and suffer much himself

16.   The particular times of accidents happening are to be found out from annual and monthly revolutions and transits

17.   Fatal will that year be to the Native's health, when in the Revolution many of the Hylegicals come to bad places of the Figure, or to the Aspects of the Infortunes.

18.   If any Planet be afflicted in an annual revolution, the effects will appear when he shall apply by body, square or opposition to the Planet that is Lord of the sign wherein he is.

19.   Diseases are for the most part of the nature of the Lord of the sixth house, or the Planet therein posited as well in Revolutions as Nativities.

20.   The Revolution of a year is one thing in time, which is the return of the Sun to the same point from the Equinoctial; another thing in the World, which is its return to the same fixed star, and yet another thing in Nativities, which is its return to its former place, but with the addition of so much of the Ecliptic as he passes through in one natural day.

Aphorisms Relating To Decumbitures, Diseases, Physic, Etc

1.   In sickness, the Ascendant shall signify the Patient, the seventh house the disease, the Luminaries the Patient's strength, the Infortunes the strength of the disease, but the eighth house has always a share in the signification.

2.   When the Moon applies to Planets of a nature contrary to that of the distemper, especially if they be Fortunes, the disease will be changed for the better.

3.   When the Moon in the beginning of a sickness (which is called the Decumbiture of the Patient) shall be either under the Sun beams or with the Dragon's Tail, Saturn or Mars, it threatens extraordinary danger, and if the party be old, even her conjunction with Jupiter, Mercury, or Venus, is not without peril; the same but nothing so grievous may be feared when she is in square or opposition to any of them but if besides all this she shall happen to have been in their places in the Patient's geniture, he will certainly die.

4. Mar   s, Jupiter, and Venus rule the blood; Mars and Sol, choler; the Moon and Venus, phlegm; Saturn and Mercury melancholy; and Mars and Mercury with the Sun, black choler.

5.   Saturn causes long diseases; Venus indifferent, Mercury various ones; the Moon such as return after a certain time, as Vertigos, Falling-sickness, etc. Jupiter and Sol give short diseases, but Mars the most acute of all.

6.   When you find the Figure at the beginning of a grievous distemper to appear much more mild and favourable than the distemper, you may conclude the disease contracts its malignity from the Nativity, the principal places falling upon some disastrous configurations.

7.   It is necessary to consider the Lunations preceding the disease and thence likewise to take indications of the Patient's condition.

8.   If you find a Person after the age of 50 years labour under strong and frequent diseases, you may conclude the significator of life in his Radix to be sorely afflicted by the body or aspects of one of the Infortunes.

9.   When the Moon is in a fixed sign physic works the less, and if in Aries, Taurus, or Capricorn it will be apt to prove nauseous and very distasteful to the Patient.

10.   In Purging, 'tis best that both the Moon and Lord of the Ascendant descend and be under the Earth: --in vomiting that they ascend.

11.   Purging, Vomiting, Bleeding, Making use of issues, etc., ought to be done while the Moon, is in moist signs, the chief of which is Pisces, the next Cancer.

12.   The significator of life in the Radix being strong in natural diseases helps very much, but in casualties, little or nothing.

13.   When the Moon is with Venus, Choler is better and more safely expelled; and when she is with Jupiter, Melancholy.

14.   Every immoderate Position of the Heavens to Persons weak and aged, brings death; to others violent accidents and grievous calamities.

15.   If a disease begin when the Moon is in opposition to the Sun, 'tis by reason of superfluity of humours; if she suffer an eclipse, the

same time 'tis for weakness of the Spirits and Vital power.

16.   The Infortunes being Oriental, cause Diseases; Occidental, defects.

17.   Venus with Saturn in the seventh and Mars elevated above them both, causes barrenness in men, and Abortions in women.

18. Sagittar   y and Gemini signify Diseases that come with falling, as Swooning, Fallingsickness, Suffocations of the womb, etc.

19.   When at the beginning of a disease the Luminaries are both with the Infortunes, or in opposition to them, the sick will very hardly escape.

20.   From the Moon's applications to the Fortunes or good aspect of the Sun, the same being neither contrary to the disease, nor afflicted, nor in the power of the Infortunes: -health may be expected, but by her going to the Infortunes of like nature with the disease, or ill beams of the Sun, death is to be feared.

21.   Cold and dry diseases, such as are naturally long, are increased by Saturn; but those that are short, hot and dry, from Mars.

22.   A conjunction of the Luminaries in Aries, causes alteration and death, if Venus and Mercury be there retrograde; the like if it happen in Scorpio or Virgo or in any humane sign; so likewise if such conjunction fall in the sixth, seventh, or eighth house of the figure of the Decumbiture within the Aspect of an Infortune, the Patient will be in great danger.

23.   Mars in the Ascendant at the Decumbiture, makes the disease, swift, violent, afflicting the upper parts and disturbing the mind; and if besides this, the dispositors of the Luminaries and Ascendant happen to be afflicted, death will follow; the like if both the Luminaries be Cadent from Angles, and not assisted by the Fortunes; but if in such a position, the Fortunes strong shall have dominion in

two places, the disease will be changed from Acute to Chronic, and the Patient at last will escape beyond hope.

24.   From the first hour of the day (or one in the morning inclusive) till six, blood predominates, whence morning sleeps become so sweet and pleasant; from thence to noon, Choler, afternoon Phlegm, and from the beginning of the Night till mid-night, Melancholy.

25.   Saturn in Fiery Signs when the Sun is 'weak causes hectic fevers; Jupiter sanguinary ones, and if Mars behold him Putrid ones; Mars in such signs gives burning fevers of all sorts; Venus ephemeral fevers, and if the rays of Mars be mixed, putrid ones from phlegm; Mercury mixed ones, but if the Moon be joined with him she makes pituitous fevers from the corruption of the humours; Saturn mixing signification with Mars, causes Melancholy fevers, and if Mars be under the Sun in the sixth or twelfth house in fiery Signs, or being so posited shall cast his beams on the Significator of life, or the Lord of the Ascendant of the Revolution, or if the Lord of the Ascendant or Significator of life apply to his aspects by direction, it occasions burning pernicious fevers and like to venomous ones; but if to these, Saturn or the Dragon's Head or Tail, or Venus Combust be added, or if these Planets shall be posited in Scorpio or Leo, the fever will be altogether pestilential.

26.   Mischievous fevers are caused when the Sun is Afflicted in Leo, but if otherwise he be fortified they seldom happen, because the matter then corrupts and is carried off, unless by chance.

27.   Watery signs threaten putrid fevers of very bad continuance if Mars (especially combust) have any rule in them, but earthly signs are altogether free from putrid fevers.

28.   It will be a fatal time to suffer amputation or lose any member when the moon is in an oblique sign under the Sun beams and

opposed by Mars.

29.   A ~tedious travail and delivery in child-birth is to be expected, when the Moon is aspected by the Infortunes, and in an oblique sign, and a Planet retrograde or slow of Motion is in the Ascendant.

30.   Venus is cold in the second degree, and moist in the third; the Moon cold in the third, and moist in the fourth; Jupiter hot in the second, and moist in the first; the Sun hot in the third, and dry in the second; Mars dry in the third, and hot in the fourth; and Saturn both cold and dry in the fourth.

31.   The special Significator of a disease is that unfortunate Planet from whom the Significator separates by a bad aspect; and the Lord of the Ascendant shows the cause of the grief if he be found anywhere unfortunate.

32.   If the Lord of the Ascendant be an Infortune the sick will be unruly, but if he be a Fortune he will readily take what is prescribed.

33.   The fifth house and its Lord, show the medicines, and their nature whether good or evil, proper or improper.

34.   As the Revolution of a year as to its ill significations, happens according to the directions from the geniture, so the decumbiture as to its worse significations is regulated by the revolution according to Lunar directions

35.   Several Planets being Significators show that the distemper is complicated of several diseases.

36.   The Significator of the disease in double-bodied signs signifies a relapse, or that it will change into some other distemper.

37. The dise   ase is desperate, when the Significator of the sick either in his Nativity or the decumbiture, has dominion in the fourth house.

38.   That sign in which the Significator of the disease is posited, and that to which he casts any aspect, show the members or parts of the

body principally afflicted.

39.   When Mercury is unfortunate he prejudices the phantasy and inward faculties, and thence threatens madness, et% but so much the worse if Mars be the Planet that affiicteth him, for then if he be in an earthy sign it threatens the Patient will make away with himself.

40.   It is a very bad sign when the Significator of the sickness is in the sixth, or the Lord of the sixth in the eighth, or the Lord of the eighth, in the sixth house.

41.   Mercury significator of a disease in aspect with Saturn, or Saturn significator in aspect of Mercury, gives suspicion of witchcraft and enchantment.

42.   A chronical disease (that is a disease which usually continues above a month) is ruled by the motion of the Sun; acute diseases (which are more sharp and violent but less lasting) by the motion of the Noon, according to whose swifter or slower motion the critical times are either hastened or retarded' the same being when the Moon comes to a sign contrary in both qualities to that in which she was in the beginning of the disease.

43.   For curing a member, the Moon and Lord of the Ascendant should be free from Impediment, the sign that governs the part ascending and the Moon posited in it, and when you think to do any good to your eyes, let the Moon be fortunate, increasing in light and by no means in a sign of the Earthly Triplicity

44.   Even the Fortunes in diseases may become Infortunes, viz., when the disease itself is of their nature, or of the nature of things by them signified, and in such case the infortunes may be said to be fortunes, for contraries are to be cured by contraries.

AphorismsConcerningElections

1.   An Election signifies nothing or very little unless it correspond with the Nativity, and time wherein you Elect.

2.   If you would have anything kept secret let the Moon be under the Sun beams when you do it

3.   Make no new clothes, nor first put them on when the Moon is in Scorpio, especially if she be full of light and beheld of Mars, for they will be apt to be tom and quickly worn out.

4.   When in an Election you cannot fit the Moon to two Planets that you have occasion for, at once, join her to some fixed star that is of the nature of them both.

5.   When you would suddenly finish a thing, place the Moon and significator in Moveable Signs, but if you would have your work last long, let them be in fixed ones, and for this reason it becomes so difficult for a man to attain to do both.

6.   The best election a man can make is the place of his habitation: for if the Ascendant of the City he dwells in be the place of his Ascendant, he will have his health well, if the MidHeaven, he will come to preferment, if it be the place of the Sun in the Nativity, he will undoubtedly obtain honour and dignities, if of Jupiter he will grow rich; if of the Moon he will be very happy in most respects there.

7.   Every man's geniture in some things agrees with, and in some differs from another's, we should therefore deal with people (as to important matters) only in things wherein their Nativities sympathize with ours, but in other things to forbear, and indeed we ought generally to avoid the society of a person the Lord of whose

Ascendant is an infortune and joined with the Dragon's Tail or any malevolent Fixed Star, for unless there be a great agreement between our Nativities they will do us some mischief, though perhaps against their will.

8.   When the significators of journies are in watery signs and the Infortunes (or the Fortunes themselves unfriendly posited) be elevated above them, the querent will be much troubled in his journies with bad weather and tempests, and note that the causes or business of journies is to be discovered from the dispositors of the significators.

9.   You may sometimes use the Infortunes as Physicians do poisons, for they produce strong effects; but use them like those, sparingly and with caution.

10.   News or reports raised and spread abroad whilst the Moon is in the beginning of Scorpio or Capricorn are generally false, but if she be with Jupiter in a masculine sign they are like to prove true.

11.   Begin not to build whilst the Moon is in Scorpio or Pieces or when a southern sign ascends, nor let the Moon or Lord of the fourth apply to a Retrograde Planet, for it threatens that such edifice shall soon fall or be ruined.

12.   At Play and in War it is said that it is considerable for s man to have his face look towards a friendly Part of Heaven, and that if both parties do so, the contest will be tedious, if neither of them, then both in battle will be much prejudiced, and in gaming there will be little won on either side, but if one of them only look that way, he will soon conquer his antagonist.

13.   In every Election let the Moon and Lord of the Ascendant be free from impediment or affliction.

14.   But if when the Moon suffers some impediment from another Planet, thou art forced on that day to make an election, let a sign ascend that is either the house or exaltation of that Planet so impediting.

15.   It is best to undertake journies when the significators are in moveable signs, for they signify celerity and return with dispatch of business, but fixed signs in such cases are very bad, so also it is if the Lord of the Ascendant or Moon happen to be in the sixth, eighth, or twelfth houses.

16.   It is an undeniable thing (in general) to deliver a petition or request to a great person when the Moon applies to Jupiter, and he is joined with the Dragon's Head in the Midheaven.

Aphorisms Relating To Eclipses AndComets

1.   In an Eclipse it is necessary to consider the strength of the Planet then ruling, for his significations will chiefly appear.

2.   Eclipses of the sun have powerful effects, and therefore if they fall upon a very flourishing and promising crop they generally damnify it, so that it scarce comes to any thing near what might have been expected.

3.   When at the time of an eclipse the significator of life in any person's Radix shall be within the Beams of the Anereta or killing Planet, or of an Infortune not friendly disposed, such native will incur extraordinary hazard of his life.

4.   In general some Eclipses of the luminaries at the time or even before they happen raise showers and rain, others great droughts, some violent winds, others earthquakes, some scarcity of the fruits of the earth, others terrible fires.

5.   A Comet usually foreshows the birth of famous persons in some time after to happen, for he is not said to be born under it (in this sense) who is born during the time of its appearance, but he that is born in that region or country subject to such an Angle or Figure, and hath his Sun and Moon in its place, or the Luminaries and the Lord of his Ascendant in cardinal signs, when the Comet rises, sets or culminates, and the like.

6.   A Comet in the East, signifies the rise of some eminent lawgiver, in the Mid-heaven, of some very powerful King, but seldom an such illustrious matter when 'tis in the West or Succedent houses.

7.   Comets when they are immoveable, signify seditions, but when moveable they denote Foreign Wars, and one Nation invading another; in Cardinal Signs the death of Princes or great men; in the ninth house, Scandal or detriment to Religion; in the tenth or twelfth houses, the pestilence or scarcity of corn; and in the eleventh house, great slaughter and destruction of Noblemen.

8.   If a Comet appear whilst a woman goes with child, if it be either in the fourth, sixth, or eighth month, such child will prove very prone to anger and quarrels, and if he be of quality, to sedition.

9.   No Eclipse whatsoever can threaten a scarcity or plague to the whole Earth, nor can the pestilence continue above four years in one place.

10.   Eclipses in the fourth house are more strong and efficacious than in the eighth or twelfth houses, and in the Ascendant more than in the ninth or eleventh.

11.   An Eclipse of the Moon extends its effects as many months, and of the Sun so many years, as it continues hours.

12.   An Eclipse has a threefold effect, first powerful by reason of the conjunction or opposition on which it happens; second general, because it slowly cools, in which respect it is extended for a long time. Thirdly power which it has from the Lord of the place wherein it happens and other positions at that time.

13.   Eclipses operate more forcibly on Cities, Provinces, and Kingdoms than on Particular persons of private condition, or even upon Kings and Princes, for their effects rather respect the multitude,

14.   When Eclipses happen or Comets appear in Earthly Signs they portend barrenness and scarcity by reason of excessive droughts; when in Watery Signs by reason of too much rain, in Airy Signs they

signify mighty winds, seditions and the pestilence, in Fiery Signs terrible Wars and slaughters.

APHORISMS TOUCHING WEATHER, METEORS, ET C

1. When Saturn passes out of one sign into another, you may expect for several days together strange Meteors and splendid sights or apparitions in the heavens.

2. When signs very different from the common course of nature appear about the Sun, or in or about the Moon, Stars. or any part of heaven, if thou observe the place where they appear, and the figure of the heaven from the beginning to the end, thou mayest come to understand what they portend.

3. The Lord of the Interlunary Figure signifies very much as to the quality of the Air, and also the Planet that beholds him, especially if they be in Cardinal Signs.

4. When Saturn is Combust in the houses of Mars, and Mars beholds him, he often begets conical figures which are seen in the air composed of vapours that ascend,, and are sips of an earthquake to ensue.

5. Saturn and Mars, and Mars and the Sun, and Mars and Mercury, cause bail; Saturn most in summer, Sol and Mercury most in autumn, and those that cause hail in these two quarters cause snow in the winter and spring.

6. Satur n with the Luminaries, Jupiter with Mercury and Mars with Venus, make an Apertio portarum or an opening of the gates, and usually cause some notable change of weather.

7. When about the beginning of winter Saturn shall dispose of the Moon, expect unusual Colds with a cloudy season and rain.

8.   Whenever Saturn is joined to the Sun the heat is remitted and the cold increased, which alone may be a sufficient testimony of the truth of Astrology.

9.   When Mars and Mercury are joined and behold the Moon or Lord of the Ascendant in the sixth or seventh house, they portend s great drought to ensue.

10.   That Star has a great efficacy on the air, to which the Moon shall be first joined after her conjunction, opposition or square with the Sun.

11.   The mixture of the beams of Jove and Mars in moist signs gives Thunder with sudden showers.

12.   Jupiter naturally raises North Winds, Saturn Easterly, Mars Western, Venus Southern, and Mercury Mixed Winds, according as he applies to other Planets.

Some Aphorisms Relating To Husbandry

1. If you prune your vines when the Moon is at full in Taurus, Leo, Scorpio, Sagittarius, neither worms nor birds will infest your grapes.

2. Graft not Trees, the Moon waning, or not to be seen, and if you shear sheep in her increase their wool will grow again the better.

3. Fruits and Wood for use should be cut in the decrease of the Moon, but if you would have Timber to keep long, fell it towards the latter end of the winter, the Moon being under the earth, and beheld by Saturn, for that will prevent its rotting, and render it exceedingly hard and durable.

4. But fire wood and what you would have grow quickly again, cut when the Moon is above the Earth in the first quarter joined either to Venus or Jupiter.

5. Sow or Plant when the Moon is in Taurus, Virgo or Scorpio in good Aspect of Saturn, but when she is in Cancer set or sow all kinds of pulse, and in Libra or Capricorn dress your gardens and trim your small trees and shrubs.

6. Saturn in fixed signs causes scarcity of corn, dear years, and the death of many men.

7. When Trees blossom they are most apt to be affected with injuries from the Heavens, for then they are like teeming women, and when they have put out their fruits like Nurses giving suck, which can endure more than when they went with child; and therefore if Eclipses happen whilst a tree is so blooming, it most times causes a scarcity of that kind of fruit that year, and indeed the plenty of corn and fruit is not much discovered from the vernal

figure or Revolution of the World, as from the temperature of the air, in moisture, dryness, or inequality, as also from the new and full Moons, and risings of the Stars; and Eclipses, especially happening then what things respectively blossom.

8. A Malevolent Planet being Lord of the year, though fortunate, generally hurts all fruits of the earth, but those particularly signified by himself.

Aphorisms Relating To General Accidents

1.   Saturn obtains Kingdoms or Supremacy of power by labour, fraud, and infamy; Mars by valour, rapine and cruelty; but Jupiter by Justice and great opinion of goodness and honesty.

2. When Saturn is in Libra and Jupiter in Cancer, great changes and alterations shall happen in the world.

3. For discovering such grand mutations we should well consider the great, mean, and lesser conjunctions of the Planets in the several Trigons, the removes of the Superiors from one sign to another, as also their applications to the fixed Stars.

4.   Likewise the changes of the *Absides* of the Planets cause mutations in governments and laws, which is a point very much to be regarded.

5. Mercury with an unfortunate Planet in the eleventh, denotes the establishment of some severe or unjust laws in the world.

6. A Conjunction of Mars and Saturn in the sixth or eighth house, especially in a humane sign, signifies a great Pestilence.

7. When in the Radix of any City Mars shall be in the Mid-heaven, the Inhabitants will be inclined to Sedition: If Saturn be there they will be very mischievous, yet very laborious.

8. If Wars be signified note the Angle of the figure wherein Mars is posited, for from that Part the Enemies shall come.

END OF THE APHORISMS OF CARDAN

Table des matières